The Care Giver

The Care Giver

AmyAnn Bauman

CONTENTS

"The grass is always greener on the other side of the fence." This is a way some people are told their life is not as bad as it seems.

I grew up on a "greener lawn" than some. From the other side, my friends and neighbors could have thought I had it easy. In many ways I did. I grew up in a Christian two-parent home. We may not have been rich, but we did not go hungry. I got most of my clothes from thrift stores (or handmade), but my needs were always met.

This saying could also teach us that the lives of others have issues we may not see from the outside. No one on this planet has a perfect life. We may not see issues or hardships in the lives of some, but I promise you they are there. Some "patches of brown" can be spotted all the way from the street, while some people do all they can to hide blemishes.

This book is about some of the problems I have faced, what I have learned from them and how God is seeing me through. I want you to know that you are not alone, though it may feel like you are at times. Even though no two people face the exact situations and feelings, there is always someone else who has faced similar problems. I have not faced the same exact struggles as you, but my prayer is that maybe some of what I have gone through can encourage and help you in what you have faced or may be facing now. I'm hoping this book will help you care more and know the ultimate Care Giver.

It is not always fun being alone. Other times being alone is all I want to do. This book is mostly about the struggles I have faced with my mother's health issues, trying to help her through some of them, and the effects it had on us both.

Just a side note:

Please do not allow imperfections of grammar or a different sense of humor take away from what you can glean from what I have written. It's sometimes easy to pay attention to the wrong people do or say instead of learning from them. I know I am flawed, so there may be unintentional mistakes in this book. I challenge you to look at what you can learn and overlook the flaws that can hinder growth.

Where It Began

Where It Began

When I was growing up my father did not have many health problems, but my mom sure did. My family at times would joke that my mother would outlive us all and survive every health issue known to mankind. That has lost it's humor for me after watching her struggle through the years.

Her health was a struggle from the time she was a child. When she was eleven her appendix had to be removed. In her early thirties she had her tubes tided and wound up having to get a hysterectomy. She's had so many physical issues and they have only worsened as she has gotten older. I'm not going to tell you every little thing that has gone wrong in my mother's life, just the parts I feel may help you understand the situation.

My mother, Cathy had my brother, Gordon when she was 15 years old. She lived a rough life for a while, turning to things like drugs and sex to find fulfillment. When she was 23, she turned to Jesus and later went to a Bible college where she met my dad, Marcus.

My mom used to have a beautiful singing voice people could hear from the other side of a crowded room. My dad was very reserved and didn't like drawing attention to himself. One day when the two were sitting together at church he asked her not to be so loud. That gave her the inspiration to sing louder! After the service was over a lady approached my mom and told her how touched she was by hearing her sing. That is when my dad knew this woman was the one he needed beside him in ministry. So, they got married when Gordon was 12, then in between five miscarriages had me and my brother, Blake.

Thinking of Others

When I was younger, I saw my mom as one of the strongest, most straight-forward women I have ever met. A lot of my care giving ways I got from her example. It was very typical for my mom to help and befriend anyone she could. I was not born wanting to make friends with many people. My mom pretty much forced me to hang out with people who were not the most popular. I definitely was not one of the popular kids growing up! I often felt awkward and out of place. Befriending and helping others helped me concentrate on other people's needs and not worry so much about my popularity.

It wasn't just me she recruited! My mom would get my dad and brothers to help with a person's tire on the side of the road. She would bring us to a soup kitchen to help us understand how blessed we are and to serve others. She would sneak money or food to someone when she could. Then she would have fun watching the person cry with joy when they would find it. Yes, we enjoy making people cry!

My mother was definitely not perfect, but she taught me how to care about others without getting paid for it or even getting credit for it. This made it easier to care for her years later. Today, I truly feel blessed when I do something for my parents.

Mistakes and Grace

My parents, like every parent, made their mistakes. Years later, as a parent myself, I now see how easy it is to mess up. This does not mean I should give up because I know I will never get everything right. It does not mean I should remember everything my parents did wrong and make it an excuse for the mistakes I make. It also should not be the reason to turn my back on my parents when they cannot take care of themselves. Instead, it should make me more understanding and gracious when I remember the mistakes they made. It also helps me realize I cannot successfully be a caregiver of any kind on my own strength or feelings. I need help from people with insight. I also need to help even when I don't feel like it.

I am sure that if you think back through your life, you could probably think of someone who forgave you when you did not deserve it or showed kindness when they did not have to. I know I have been blessed with people in my life who have been patient with me when I was being difficult. It is those types of situations and people that enrich others and make the world a better place.

We have a daily choice to make. Are we going to hold on to bitterness and excuses or be generous and inspiring? A teacher at the Bible school I attended used to say, "You can choose to be bitter or better." I think we all want to make this world a better place, we just don't always like the effort it requires. Honestly, when you first start giving up bitterness it can be tough, but I promise you, it is so worth it. As we surrender our bitterness and frustrations it's like losing excess weight. It's so freeing and makes me wonder why I didn't do it sooner!

Difference Between Parents

My dad would do things with us that were on the more active side like jumping on the trampoline and skating. My mom did more indoor activities like crafts and baking. When her body would cooperate with her, she would help with yard work, but she usually did things on the less active side. My dad would also do indoor things with us like games and puzzles, but he also would do the physically challenging activities my mom was not always able to do. He would tell stories from his imagination, and she would read books with fun voices for each character.

Whether they were inside or outside, my parents were definitely not lazy. They taught me how to work hard and not expect handouts. They both were very gifted artists in different ways. My dad could make drawings look realistic and taught our high school art class. He made some cool-looking comics too. My mom did more cartoon type pictures and taught cake decorating. She actually had a cake business and made some pretty awesome looking cakes. They both are very creative people in very different ways.

Why I Wrote This Chapter

I have changed a lot since I was a kid and so have my parents. A lot has happened since then. I will explain deeper in different chapters of the events that have helped shape me and my parents into who we are today. This chapter of our lives is very important. Without this chapter you would not be able to understand the kind of effect these physical limitations have impacted our lives. It is only by remembering this chapter that I am able to understand all that my mom had to give up. And she had no choice.

She wasn't able to do some of the things with us that my dad did, like bowling. Now, she can barely turn pages in a book or get food from the oven. As a grandmother, she is not able to bake for her grandkids like she used to. She can no longer scrapbook or make their birthday cards. She can't sew them dresses like she did for me. She cannot do the things that used to give her such enjoyment. In understanding this, I am more equipped to empathize with her when she's having a rough day.

I know as a Christian she should find her joy in Jesus, but that doesn't take away all the pain and loss she feels. There's a reason the Bible says things like "be angry and do not sin." (Eph. 4:26) The Bible also says that "Jesus wept." (John 11:35) Jesus was the perfect man and He hurt for others. He didn't want to go through pain, but was willing to if it would rescue the ones He loves. He showed us how to love by surrendering Himself. (Mark 14:36)

There is nothing wrong with the feelings we have. It's what we do with those feelings that count. Remembering other people's feelings does not excuse their bad behavior, but does help us understand the behavior and makes it easier to show grace and mercy.

Anyone can say, "Let Jesus be your strength" and "Don't stress over things you cannot fix." Not many act on this advice. That's a shame, because I've noticed that the people who act on these beliefs actually have true joy in a gloomy circumstance. They have hope because they have something to look forward to in the long run.

It is easy to say, "Just do what you can with what you have." It is not easy to have things taken from you. This helps me understand what my kids go through when a cherished toy goes missing or gets destroyed. This helps me understand someone whose memory is fading. This also prepares me to help someone who can no longer dress themselves.

Something to think about:
Imagine with me for a moment that you only have one vehicle. This vehicle helps you get to work, see your friends and family, and helps you carry your groceries home. One day your car is taken away and you do not have enough money or credit to buy or rent another car. Now that you have no car and no way of getting another, how do you feel? Hold on to that feeling for a moment. This is how some people feel when

something is taken from them. It doesn't have to be a car, it could be a leg or use of their hands, you name it.

I'll tell you something that is true. Something being taken from you would not make you less valuable. With that in mind, we should never value people by the things they own or the abilities they currently have. We can help someone feel valuable by spending time with them. Maybe write a note saying you were thinking of them and hope they are doing well. Maybe you could give some words of affirmation by giving a compliment. Do you know someone who is lonely? Why not find a way to make them feel special today?

Having your car taken would not make you less capable of having a conversation. It would not mean you require less love and patience than anyone else. You actually would need more. It might make you angry with the person who took it (which explains why some people are mad at God, they might be holding Him responsible). It might make you feel vulnerable, because you have to get a ride from someone else. It would make you less mobile and more irritable.

Please remember this when you talk to someone who is less mobile than you or less mobile than they use to be. Whatever the situation, having to rely on others is not easy. It is especially difficult when that person you're depending on is unreliable or impatient.

Challenge Extended

My challenge for both you and myself is to remember the person you are talking to or helping is no less valuable than you are. We need to be dependable. We need to be kind and respectful. Getting to know the person is a great way to understand what they truly need from you and a way to show them you actually care.

We need to be understanding without patronizing the people in our lives that are no longer able to do things. Imagine yourself not being able to do those things, especially for those who will never be able to do them again this side of heaven. I imagine it'd be a bigger struggle than getting out of a long-term relationship. I imagine it being very frustrating, depressing even.

I hate being sick. I hate asking for help. It can be very humbling and, at times, humiliating. That helps me understand a little bit more how I can be a help to my mom. She does not need me to treat her like a baby. She's an adult, so why would I look at her like I would a kid? She's my mother. The Bible tells me to honor my parents, not treat them like an inconvenience.

Side note: I do understand as some people get older and start to lose their memory, they need to be watched closer. As you are watching, never lack kindness or respect. Those two things go a long way with the people you are helping and the people watching you help them.

So, we need to:
show respect.
stay positive (especially in a negative situation).
not wait for them to ask us to do what needs to be done.

Just like it would be nice for people to offer you a ride when your car is in the shop, it is nice not having to ask for someone to clean your house when your body is less mobile. Now, this is going to be different with every situation. When my mom started not being able to do as much, I didn't want to overstep my bounds, so I asked if she was okay with me doing the dishes and laundry. Now, when I am at my parents' house and see there's a load of laundry in the hamper, I no longer ask if she needs me to do it. If I am physically able to do something I see needs done, I do it. Now, I know she needs me to, and she knows I am doing it out of love.

Doing acts of service is one of my main love languages and it is a way I can show her and others the love of Christ. After all she did for me as a kid, it is the least I can do for her.

Nursing Home

When I only had three kids, I took them to visit a friend of mine at a nursing home. I saw a lot of different emotions as we sat with my friend in the entrance area. I saw a lot of pain, probably physical and emotional. There were a couple who looked angry. Most of them just looked lonely. Some places like this are nicer than others, but this place was not a place I would want to live. While we were there my oldest, who was around four years old, started talking to anyone who listened.

She is very outgoing and doesn't know a stranger. She had no inhibitions whatsoever! There was one person who looked annoyed by her, but everyone else looked to be enjoying her chatter. I saw a few tears on smiling faces, and it caused me to have a few of my own! At such a young age Mikayla saw what a lot of people skip over, the fact that those people were worth talking to and getting to know. Their age and mobility were not a factor for her wanting to love on them and communicate with them. They still have value. Sometimes our busy schedules get in the way of what is important in life. It sometimes takes an immobility to help us realize people are what matter in the end.

When you are caring for someone, try to never look at them as just a job. This could probably be easy to do if it's your actual career. I want to encourage you to see the face of someone God has created with equal value as me and you. Think of what they need from you and not just what is convenient or a job requirement. Do your best to go the extra mile.

Think of the real needs of this person. Do they need you to be quiet? Do they need companionship? They may need to know that God is real, He loves them, and is not allowing things to happen out of spite.

To those of you in a situation where you are physically limited,

I do not know the reason God lets some things happen, but I do know that He has a plan to work all things together for our good as we love and trust Him. (Romans 8:28) It doesn't say He makes all things feel good, but it does say He makes things work together for our good. I know He wants to help you with your problems.

The Bible says in Matthew 11:28-30, you can go to Jesus when you are tired and weary, and He will give you rest. It says to let Him walk and work beside you and to learn from Him. He is willing to help you with your burdens. There is no better teacher or friend.

One thing that sometimes helps me when I am faced with unpleasant situations is knowing this life is about the next life. Everything we do for God will last forever! When it feels like this pain will never end, take courage because eventually this life will end, and we will be given a better body than we have now. Eventually, God will make all things clear to us and we will be able to understand all the whys and why nots. (1 Corinthians 13:12)

2

Caring From Afar

My First Mission Trip

When my brother, Blake and I were teenagers we went on summer mission trips with a ministry called Teen Missions International. It's a ministry that trains teenagers to be missionaries. Each group would get trained in Florida at what is called the Lord's Boot Camp for two weeks, go to their mission location for about a month, then get debriefed for a few days before going home.

My first trip was when I was 14 years old. My team's name was Music Fest II. We went around the United States to different music festivals promoting Teen Missions and helping with things like parking and children's outreach. We would do different dramas and puppet shows at the festivals and at parks and camps.

While kids are with Teen Missions, they are not allowed to have cell phones or other electronics (which wasn't a big deal back then). Therefore, letters were the way to let your loved ones know how you were doing and about the adventure you were on. It was also how you found out what's going on at home while you were away.

Most teams stayed in one place during their mission time, but my team didn't stay in the same place for very long. Because we traveled so much, we didn't always get the letters that were sent to us. I didn't get very many letters the month we were away and it made me a bit sad thinking no one had spent time writing me. I didn't know it at the time, but my mom wrote me a few times every week. I simply hadn't received them.

The lesson here is, God sends us messages we don't always get. Sometimes we just don't pay attention and then wonder why He isn't doing anything for us. It's like not checking the mailbox and wondering why the mail never comes. He is faithful even if we don't always understand what He is doing.

In Mark 4 the disciples went through a really bad storm and got a bit upset with Jesus for sleeping. They asked Jesus if He even cared that they were going to drown! Jesus then calmed the wind and sea, turned to them and asked why they were afraid and had no faith in Him. It is so easy to forget the goodness we have experienced when we are in those "storms" of life.

Letters at Debrief

When we got back to Florida for debrief I had a big pile of letters waiting for me. Most of them were from my mom! Some of her letters did not make sense, because I didn't get them all. One said something about doctors using her as a pincushion. Another said the doctor took out the stitches and she would have an impressive scar. My imagination was going all over the place! I found out later she had thyroid cancer and she had to get her thyroid taken out.

Back home, my mom didn't realize I didn't understand what had happened while I was away. (Honestly, I didn't even know what or where a thyroid was until years later!) So, when she would talk about things, I would usually be lost trying to understand what was going on. This is how it is sometimes when people start reading the Bible. The books are not in chronological order, so it can be a little confusing at times. It really helped me understand the Bible better when I read it in the order things happened, just like I understood her letters more when I was told about her surgery.

Different Family

After I got home I was informed that I would be moving in with one of the home school families from our weekly co-op. I stayed with them for a school year. I would go to their house Sunday or Monday and usually come home after co-op on Friday. There was a mix of emotions, because at the time I was not given a choice or a reason. I did not know why I had to go live with people outside of my family. I was not thrilled to go there, but in the long run it was good for me.

Sometimes things happen and we are not given a choose or a reason. Or maybe, we were and we just were not paying attention. Sometimes, what is best for us is not knowing until after we have said yes. The best way to be content and have peace is when we walk in obedience to God and just trust Him. What an adrenaline rush that can be! It can be scary and sometimes painful, but God knows what is needed in order to refine and renew our hearts and minds.

Help Prepare

If children are involved in the mix of needing care or caring for someone, please communicate enough with them that they are not continually left in the dark. Sometimes that can be scarier than anything. You do not need to scar them with gory details, just let them know enough of the plan that they are not constantly caught off guard. If possible, give them a little bit of a heads up before moving them. That will help them be better mentally and physically prepared.

It is best to not overwhelm people, especially children, by giving too much information at once. Just like it takes your body time to digest food, it sometimes takes time to mentally digest life-changing information. I was not the kind of kid that would ask questions, I just went along with what I was told to do. If someone did not offer information, I would just try to figure things out instead of asking. A lot of kids can become that way after a while of not being able to trust the situation they are in.

So, when you are giving kids information, give enough so they know what to expect, but not so much that it is overwhelming. If they are about to face something challenging or maybe scary, you could let them know that God is everywhere and can hear them when they talk to Him and they are not alone. You could help boost their confidence by pointing out their strengths and that God would not leave them and would give them strength to deal with whatever comes next. Whether a person is young or old, we all need kindness, respect , and a touch of inspiration.

Teach while being Taught

Because my mom was having health issues, she did not always teach at the weekly co-op like the other moms did. Every family needed to contribute, so I taught sign language classes for a few years. I didn't mind at all. I found out I like teaching! I found the best way to learn is to teach. I wound up being friends with more parents than students. I guess that's one way to have friends who are more mature! Teaching one or two classes each week meant less classes as a student, which meant sometimes more and sometimes less work I had to do. It helped motivate me to stay more organized than I probably would have been and a better student for the other teachers' sake.

Sometimes being in a family means we need to pick up the slack of our family members. We all need help from time to time, so it is good to not begrudge someone who is unable to do something. Sometimes people have to step down from something so others can step up. Me having to step up was actually a blessing to me, because through those classes I learned how much I like teaching. Those classes I taught in high school gave me the confidence I needed later in life to teach other types of classes. God works things together for our good even if we don't see it at the time.

Oh, Brother!

Not long after I moved back home, we found out my sister-in-law, Adelle was pregnant with her second baby boy. She had gestational diabetes and was struggling with her pregnancy. So I helped with my three-year-old nephew, Cody for a while during the toughest parts of the pregnancy and a little after baby Tyler was born. They lived about three hours away from my parents, so I would stay with Gordon and Adelle for chunks of time. I was cramming two years of school into one, so I would wake up around 3am to get my schoolwork done before Cody woke up and do some more during his nap.

Sometimes helping someone is taking care of someone else. Being pregnant is not easy. Being pregnant while taking care of little kids is definitely not easy. If you know someone who is pregnant and has young children, you could be a huge blessing by offering to baby-sit or simple things like picking up their curbside for them. It doesn't take a huge gesture to be a huge blessing.

Another Family

When I was sixteen I moved in with a different family from co-op. I think my mom's goal was to have someone help me and keep me accountable with my schooling while sticking with my Friday co-op. Some places I stayed were better for me than others.

I hated change and did not like being tossed around without being communicated with. But like I said, I wasn't going to ask questions. I also wasn't going to tell anyone when I was struggling. That brings me back to "the grass is always greener on the other side of the fence." It might look green, but there might be thorns you don't see. We do not always see when someone is struggling, so let's not give them more to struggle with. A smile, a kind word, and someone simply holding the door for us seem like such small things, but make a big difference.

Think of the Children

If you are caring for a child that is not used to being with you or your family, be very patient with them and understand that this is all new to them. Here are some of the things that were different with the families I stayed with and my own family:

The type of food they ate and times they ate it

The schedule and how tightly they stuck with it

The bed (or cot or couch) I slept on

The music they listened to and TV they did or did not watch

The amount of children (and noise level) in the home

The cleanliness of the house

The amount of free time and work expected from each person

The amount of adult supervision

These are just examples of what may be different. Be understanding, but stick with a healthy amount of structure. Children need healthy food, a safe place to sleep, and some type of schedule, especially during school. Be positive, but not fake. Sound overwhelming? Please don't stress, just think of where the kid(s) came from and what they need now. Some people need more of a listening ear. Others might not feel like talking, but need to know there is someone who will be there and are dependable. Some may not have ever been given concrete boundaries and may want to test the ones you give.

I used to get so frustrated with my kids when they would do something they knew was wrong and look at me with a face that said, "What are you going to do about it?". Children will test the boundaries they have been given to see if they can trust the person who gave it. When a kid sees you mean what you say, it makes it easier to trust what you say. And when they see that you truly care about them in your words and actions, they will be able to trust you and feel safe with you.

So, when kids test the limits, they are not doing it because they hate you. They want to know if they can still depend on you. Everyone needs love and accountability. Love them enough to give an appropriate consequence when they break the rules and praise them when they do a job well done.

Never overreact when they confide in you. If you cannot control your actions with the feelings you have, how can they trust you with advice and their feelings? They need to know they can tell you anything. When you overreact it tells them you cannot handle what they have to say. They need someone safe to go to with their feelings and things that might be going on in their life. If they don't feel safe with you or feel like you can't handle what they have to say, they might try someone else to feel safe or understood. That someone else may not have their best interest in mind.

No one is perfect, but it's usually easy to see when someone is making an effort and actually cares. You may not get everything right, but don't give up or loose hope. Think of how you would feel in the other person's situation. Some people need more time and effort in order to see the difference you are making. Hang in there, you are making some type of difference. Just make sure it's a positive one.

The mom of the first house I stayed in was so sweet. She would let me help her in the garden and cook with her. She was a very patient person, and still is. I did not tell her until twenty years later the effect she had on me. Every time I make chicken I think of the kind soul that allowed me to stay with her family and I praise the good Lord for putting her in my life. Whether you see results or not, know that what we do for Christ is eternal in us and the people we care for.

3

3 Strokes for 16 Candles

Stroke One!

When I moved back in with my parents at sixteen, a lot had changed. My mother's health was still an issue, but I am so glad now that I was home for this chapter of our life. I wasn't happy at the time, but now I can see the good that came from these bad situations. Not only did it give me more material for this book(!), but this chapter showed me the extent of my bitterness and how to treat people like it is the last time I'll see them.

There was a conversation that took place that year which changed more in my life than I can divulge in this book. My mom said something that would have seemed harmless to someone listening in. My response, however, was swift and hit in a tender spot. I did not physically touch my mom, but the words I used hit her strait in the heart. The saying, "sticks and stones can break my bones, but words will never hurt me" are completely untrue. My words were very hurtful and to this day (almost twenty years later) I regret them.

After I said what I said to my mom, she fell from her desk chair onto the living room floor and would not respond. My first thought was that I had just killed my mother and was going to jail. I did not know what to do. I took a deep breathe and felt for a pulse. Thankfully, I found one. I attempted to arouse her. Honestly, I don't remember what I said or did to finally get her to wake up. I just remember thinking my mother almost died and the words I said were to blame.

We found out later that the episode in the living room was most likely a stroke. That was one of three strokes my mom had when I was the only other person around. All three happened in less than a year. Needless to say, I did not feel comfortable being alone with my mom for quite some time after these happened. I was convinced I would be the one to find her body when her soul left it. Every time I would go into her room I would brace myself to find her corpse.

Lesson 1

No matter how upset you are, controlling your tongue is very important. Think before you speak. I once was given a card with the acronym for the word think on it. Before we speak we need to T.H.I.N.K. Is what I'm about to say True? Is it Helpful? Is it Inspiring? Is it Necessary? And last, but not least, is it Kind? If the answer is no, than it should not be said. Once you say something it can never be unsaid. I once saw a children's pastor demonstrate this with a tube of toothpaste. Trying to unsay something is like trying to get the toothpaste back in the tube. Once you say something it can never be unsaid.

Instead of saying things we'll most likely regret, lets be kind and say things that we can be proud of later. One of my family's verses is Ephesians 4:32, "Be kind to one another, tenderhearted, forgiving one another, as God in Christ forgave you."

I wish I could tell you that since this event took place, I have never again said anything mean or stupid, but unfortunately I have. I am not perfect and God does not expect me to be. But as I become better friends with God and spend more time with Him the more He helps me think differently (Romans 12:2). The more I think like Him, the more I act and speak like Him. I am never going to be perfect like Him, but He has started a wonderful work on my heart and mind and has promised to keep working on me. (Phil 1:6)

Stroke Two!

The second stroke she had was while she was driving! Thankfully, she was able to pull out of traffic onto the side of the road. And thankfully, we had gotten a cell phone not long before this happened.

An ambulance was called and arrived. After they loaded her up, I sat in the passenger side of the ambulance. That was quite the experience! There were times people would not move out of the way. It helped me understand what the ambulance drivers deal with every day. So just a friendly reminder, if an emergency vehicle is behind you, do them a favor and move out of the way! If it was you or your loved one, you would want others to clear a path for you.

Lesson 2

I can look at the fact that my mom had another stroke and think I have a horrible life because something horrible just happened. Or maybe, I can concentrate on the fact that she was able to pull over, so we did not cause a wreck. Plus, if she would have had the stroke a year earlier, I probably would not have been there to call for help and I would not have had a phone to call with. God's timing might be frustrating sometimes, but He knows what He's doing. Remember how much He does do and that His plans are worth waiting on.

I do not understand everything God does, but I am starting to understand His loving care. I do not always understand why He allows some things to happen, but I know He will turn everything I hand over to Him into something beautiful. Some of the things He allows to happen is for my eternal growth or the growth of someone around me. I don't always feel like it's worth it, but I know it is, or eventually will be.

Stroke Three!

Her third stroke also happened while she was driving. This time, she actually drove herself all the way to the hospital! I ran for a wheelchair and called my father to let him know where we were. That was quite the experience! She reacted really weird to the medication the doctor gave her. She was saying all kinds of strange things like, "My cat will eat your dog!" and "Watch out, Amy, he's right behind the curtain!"

After a while of going back and forth between saying funny things and sleeping, something not so funny happened. Her heart rate started being very inconsistent. The doctor and one or two nurses came in. Then the line that usually goes up and down on the monitor went flat and there was a long beep sound from the machine. Her heart had stopped. A little bit later I heard the nurse and doctor talking. The doctor said what time it was and was about to say something else when the long beep started beeping again and the strait line once again started moving. I heard the time-watching doctor say, "Just kidding!"

As a sixteen-year-old, I did not know how to respond. I just quietly watched. My mom didn't remember any of this. The doctor had given her the wrong medication and it had a really bad effect on her. A lesson there is, try your best to take notes when dealing with medical issues and have the doctor write out the diagnosis and what meds and treatment they give. Pay attention to allergies of people you are taking care of and any abnormal behavior they are having.

After my mom received the correct medicine at the hospital, the doctor told her that if she were to have another stroke, she could wind up paralyzed. That got our attention! She could live in fear of having another stroke or enjoy each day God gives her. Even though she had three strokes in so short a time, to my knowledge she has not had any since. She has had other problems, but so far, the strokes have finished their swinging.

Lesson 3

While you're driving, show some grace. The other person might not be having a stroke, but they might be dealing with things in, or with, their car that you might not be aware of. I hate it when people don't use their blinkers. Lately, I tell myself they might have used it and the bulb has gone out. Even if they don't have a good reason for making a mistake, showing kindness will do more for us all than yelling and showing them a finger would.

Summery

If I were to combine these three lessons in my life, here would be the result. When I look at the blessings instead of the problems in my life, it helps me be more positive and eventually helps be motivational to others. When I am speaking life to myself and others it helps me and those around me to live more richly. When I am not assuming the worse of others, it might help bring out the best in them and me.

When some people are faced with death, they start looking at all the things they regret or the things they did not get to do. If you knew you were about to die, what would you change in the time you have left? Would you make things right with God or someone in your life? Would you make sure your loved one knows you love them? Instead of waiting around for a close to death experience like my mom did, why not live each day as if it were your last, because one day it will be.

As I finished high school I worked at What-A-Burger full time. My dad would drive me to work and wait for his shift to start and when I got off I would work on school work while waiting for his shift to end. Of course, on Friday I would go to co-op. Nothing too exciting happened with my mom until years later.

4

Allergic to Soap

After High School

After I graduated high school, I went to a Christian summer camp, where I finally made things right with the Lord. After I surrendered my life to God I felt like a completely different person. I started acting differently. I started forgiving people who hadn't even asked for forgiveness. I started laughing when things weren't even funny. I had true joy. I didn't feel like an imposter any longer and that felt amazing!

A short time later, I went on my third trip with Teen Missions. This time to China! After that summer I stayed with my parents for a couple months, then moved to Florida to attend Teen Missions' Bible school. I was mostly in Florida for two years and spent my one year of internship in South Africa.

After my three years of Bible school were finished, I stayed with my parents for half a year to get supporters to be in ministry fulltime. I moved back to Florida to join staff at Teen Missions. During the summers I would lead teams and teach puppeteer and ballooning classes at the Lord's Boot Camp. People started calling me the puppet lady! It was a lot of hard work and I absolutely loved it! During the rest of the year I was in charge of making sure all the teams and bases around the world had the evangelism equipment they needed.

My mom would worry about me if I went more than a couple days without contacting her. She always wanted to make sure I was alright. She really struggled with me being in different countries and her not being able to see me. If you have a parent like this and you are not living with them, it could help them to just text them when you do not have a lot of time to just say you love them and reassure them you are doing well. Maybe even include something you are learning or something that was a recent blessing to you.

Married Missionary

While I was on staff I got married to a man I met at Bible school. His name is Adam. I got pregnant with our first daughter, Mikayla right away. Teaching puppet classes at boot camp while pregnant with no air conditioning was definitely character building!

When I was around 16 weeks along in my pregnancy, I was showing the choreography for a puppet song to a group of teenagers. In the middle of the song I stopped abruptly when I felt a precious little flutter! The kids asked what was going on and I told them I could feel her moving! Some of the kids were excited, and others were confused because they didn't think I looked pregnant. When they came back a month later for debrief, I had developed a baby bump. It was fun to share those moments and help them see the beauty of life. It was exciting to introduce the returning teenagers to the baby who caused the stir in puppet class!

Someone and Something New

After Mikayla was born my parents came to Florida to meet their first granddaughter. They loved holding her and I really enjoyed sharing my life and ministry with them. While they were staying with us, they would help me with the baby and cleaning around the house. I had baby Mikayla by C-section so I wasn't suppose to lift anything heavier than 10 pounds, so my dad would lift the car seat anytime we went anywhere.

One day while my mom was helping me with dishes, her hands started tingling. We thought she might have been allergic to the dish soap I had. What we thought was just an allergy to dish soap was actually the beginning stage of neuropathy.

Michigan and Miscarriage

Adam and I stayed with Teen Missions until Mikayla was a year old. We then moved to Michigan where we became relief house parents at Baptist Children's Home. Being a relief house parent meant we would go to the houses and the regular "parents" would leave for a few days. It gave them a chance to work on personal things and catch up on their rest. We would go to three houses each month.

That was one of the toughest years of my life. Two days before Christmas I had a miscarriage. I didn't know what to do. I was waiting for Christmas to tell my husband and family about the baby, so when I lost him/her I didn't say a word to anyone for about a year. Yes, you read that right, it took about a year for me to talk about it with Adam.

This was not an easy time. I was only around 7 weeks along, but I was already dreaming of the name, what it would be like with two babies, and how my daughter would be as an older sister. Part of me shut down emotionally. I got pregnant with my next baby not long after loosing my heaven baby. I was scared that the same thing would happen again. I am so thankful it didn't.

If you are the loved one of a woman who just lost a baby, I am so sorry. My advice is not to try to tell her everything is okay. Do not try to fix her or the situation. Simply let her know you are there for her. Be there for her when she needs a hug or needs a listening ear. This helps more than you might think.

Be patient, always. Everyone grieves differently. It could take her longer than you think it should. True healing usually takes time, so don't rush. God never promised us a problem-free life, but He did say He would never leave us and would care for us. Cast all your cares on Him, because He cares for you (1 Peter 5:7). I read somewhere once that "casting" your cares means to roll upon. God wants us to roll our heavy burdens on Him. He wants to ease your burden and help you with your struggles. (Matthew 11:28-30)

Struggle

With this pregnancy, like the others, my stomach didn't like holding food down. I still had to cook for the kids in the houses we went to. One of the kitchens had an aroma that my stomach would always react to! Because I couldn't keep food down, my energy level was not very high. I had a one-year-old I had to take care of, training every week, and a lingering sense of loss I could not shake.

Moving to different people's houses as a teenager helped me be more understanding with what the kids in the children's home were going through. I truly believe God sometimes allows us to go through things, not just to build our character and help our faith grow, but to also help others in their struggle and know how to pray for them better. God can help make those horrible experiences into a connection between us and someone else who needs direction or encouragement. So, we can choose to wallow in self-pity, or we can make the world a better place.

I was struggling with the loss of my baby and the food I kept losing, but seeing the situations of some of the kids in the home helped me remember at times I am not the only person with difficulties. So not only did I hopefully help them, they also helped me. "Iron sharpening iron" so to speak.

Prepping Big Sister

Eventually, my mom came for a visit and brought a surprise for the sister-to-be. My mom wanted to help Mikayla understand what it would be like to have a baby around, so she brought a somewhat realistic looking baby doll. My mother taught Mikayla how to hold the baby and let her know how important it was to be gentle. Mikayla would sing to the baby and put a blanket on her and tuck her in! It was so sweet watching her pray with her little baby doll and kiss her good night!

If you know someone expecting a baby sibling, a prep baby doll worked wonderfully for us and is a great gift idea. It also gave Mikayla a baby to take care of when I was taking care of her little sister. She would nurse her baby while I nursed mine.

5

Helping Parents While Parenting

Back to Texas

When I was in my last trimester, we left the children's home. We wound up moving in with my parents in Texas for about eight months. During that time, we had our second daughter, Haley. Mikayla slept in her own room next door to ours. Baby Haley slept in the same room as me and Adam, it was a little cramped!

When you have house guests it can be a challenge, just like not living in your own house can have it's challenges. I didn't want to add stress to my parents, so I would cook and clean throughout each day. I did my best to keep their house the way they liked it.

Having a house guest can be a challenge, but having a house guest who never cleans up after themselves can be maddening! If you are living with someone, please do not expect them to clean up after you (unless you are maybe paying them to do so). Strive to be a blessing and a joy to have around. You could help with things like dishes, laundry, and sweeping if you are physically able to.

I saw a sign at a shop in San Antonio that said, "If you sleep on it...make it. If you wear it...hang it up. If you drop it...pick it up. If you eat out of it...wash it. If you open it...close it. If you empty it...fill it. If it rings...answer it. If it needs you...be there. If it cries...love it." Do not wait to be asked, be a blessing always. You can either give reasons for eviction or be a blessing and help ease that person's burden.

Stay-At-Home

My parents and husband worked outside the home, so I was the only one home all day every day with the kids. It actually takes more willpower to do things around the house when that is where I am all day long. When the place we live is also a full-time nonpaying job, it can feel a little cramped and overwhelming at times! At times, I felt like a prisoner! Other times, I couldn't believe how blessed I was to have such beautiful treasures to take care of.

If you are a stay-at-home parent/caregiver, please know you have a very important job. There may be times you don't think anyone appreciates you or sees what all you do. I promise you; you are not alone, and I do know the One who sees. God sees every dish you wash and every diaper you change. He sees when you are doing your best and when you put others before yourself. On days you crawl into bed without a shower, because you are just too tired, God sees the effort you have put into your day. Matthew 25:40 says that when we do things for people, we are serving Jesus.

There are days I get tired of cleaning pee off the floor or sheets. There are days I hate hearing fighting and wonder if my children will ever stop being mean to each other. Eventually, it all will end. When it does, we will not be asked what we went through or how much we had to deal with. We are going to answer for and be remembered for the responses/ reactions we give.

Family Neighborhood

We were very blessed to be able to stay with my parents while we got on our feet. But I think it's safe to say, we all liked having our own houses again. We didn't go far, only one house over. That wound up being a good thing, because we were able to help each other when needs arose. My aunt lives next door as well, so we also had her help when I got pregnant again. They were able to help me when I was having pregnancy issues. I was able to help them with their yards when I wasn't pregnant and I was there those times my mom couldn't do something because of her hands.

Pros and Cons

Living with family so close has its cons. When my kids are being loud outside in the morning, it sometimes wakes my mom up prematurely. When my yard needs mowed or my kids leave their toys around the property, I will eventually hear about it from someone.

We don't always get to pick our pros and cons, but they will both show up throughout our lives. We do however, get to choose which we focus on the most. My side of the family might be able to see more of my kids' mistakes because they live so close, but they also have at times helped my kids with those mistakes.

One time my third daughter, Lila was becoming a miniature Houdini ninja! I did not know she had figured out how to, not only open the back door, but also unlock it and close it back without making a sound! The first time she did it, she made it all the way to my parents' gate (about an acre away)! A couple times, she escaped and went over to my mom's house. I'm surprised I don't have more gray hairs than I do!

If you search for something negative, you will find it every time. If you search for something positive, you will eventually find it. Sometimes positives can be harder to find, but as you get in the habit of looking for them, it gets easier to spot the blessings in our lives.

Oh, the Pain!

By this chapter in our lives, my mom's neuropathy had gotten to the point where it hurt to do some things like wear shoes all day and handle things that vibrated like the hand mixer, sewing machine, and razor to cut my dad's hair. It gradually got to the point where putting shoes on at all took all day to recover from and icing a cake was just too painful. She eventually had to stop doing some of the things she loved and counted as a part of her identity.

One of the things she stopped doing was putting on shoes. She put on shoes as little as possible. Therefore, she stopped working and going to church. Instead of going to the store, she would order curbside and my father would pick it up after he got off work.

For those of you who do not know what neuropathy is, neuropathy is a type of nerve damage. With my mom, it started off with tingling in her hands. Eventually it moved to her feet as well and caused numbness, burning and a lot of pain. At first it was an occasional pain. Then it was an occasional relief from pain. After a while it grew to unbearable pain without relief. It also got to the stage where she lost feeling in her feet. She has to be careful when she's walking and needs to check her feet for things like splinters daily, because if there is an infection that goes unnoticed, it could cause issues leading to amputation.

Not trying to be a downer, just showing you the issues that people with neuropathy face. It is not something that fixes itself. The person has to be very proactive. A good diet helps things not go down hill as quickly. In some cases, a good diet can reverse nerve damage, but not for the type of neuropathy my mother has. This has been an extremely hard decade to say the least.

Most people cannot touch ice for long periods of time, but people with really severe neuropathy cannot touch things that are cold, hot, spiky, or even sticky. Because my mom no longer could touch cold things, my dad and I would crack the ice trays for her. Because she couldn't touch hot things, she stopped baking (that included her cake business). Because she couldn't touch sticky things, she stopped scrap booking. She couldn't turn pages in a book, so she stopped reading. She got to the point where she was surrounded by the things she could no longer do.

Minimize

One thing that had helped me manage my house better was getting rid of all the things we did not use. This meant less storage space needed, less to put away, and more space for my kids to roam.

Some of you may be thinking, "I don't have time to declutter, I have enough to do around my house." I thought it would be a time-consuming activity as well, but instead of cleaning around something, I would get rid of it and could actually clean the whole floor and counter. It eventually saved me a lot of time and stress. Instead of constantly picking up toys and finding spots for things, I would give them to people that might like them. That wound up being a blessing for both of us. Win, win!

It doesn't have to be an all-day event. Some days I would just have a five-minute time of finding trash and thrift store items. Some days I would make it my goal to fill one box to get rid of or maybe just one item. The more I get rid of, the less stress my house is to clean and be in. The same was true for my mother's house.

Every once and a while, when I would help my mom clean or cook, she would tell me something else she wanted me to get rid of for her. Even though some things were hard to see her part with, I was very proud of her. It wasn't the item itself I was sad to see go, but the ability I knew meant so much to her.

Helping Others Minimize

Some things were extremely sentimental, and I had to be respectful with how I handled them. Never treat something disrespectfully when you know it means something to the person giving it up. Please be understanding. Giving up a sewing machine and all the buttons and materials when you cannot use them is the logical thing to do. But, it can also be heartbreaking. The reason it sometimes is so hard to get rid of things is the feeling of giving up on the thing it represents. For example: the reason someone might have a hard time getting rid of a sewing machine is, they feel like they are admitting they will never sew again. For some, it's admitting defeat. For others, it's giving up a dream.

Some of the abilities my mother could no longer do meant a lot to her. How can a person show their creativity if they have no way of making the things in their mind? Sometimes it feels like things we are able to do is who we are. I wonder if it felt like her identity was being stripped clean from her. If this is you, please know that God did not make you for the things you are able to do. He made you to bring glory to Him, find your strength in Him, and help strengthen others. He will never stop loving you or listening to you based on your abilities, but He does want to help you through your struggles.

Being the Parent

Helping run two households was very tiring some days. There were times that it felt like I was walking on a tightrope. I didn't want to neglect my kids or marriage while helping my parents. And I didn't want to overwhelm my mother with my rowdy children over at her house too much. I want my kids to grow up caring about others. What better way to do that than to take care of someone right in front of them?

Some days my mom is in so much physical pain, she cannot help but cry out. When my kids would see that, they would ask if she was okay. That would cause her to cry from emotions. I did not want to make her feel worse by having my girls over in times she was at her breaking point. Eventually, I had to just play it by ear and pray that God would help me know when and what to do for my kids and for my mom.

Homeschool Mama

I home school my children. Some days we would do a subject or two at Meemaw's house. I would get each kid started with what they needed to do at the table and start a load of laundry. I would check on them between tasks. Some days we would school at home and I would keep my phone close by, then go to my mom's house when she needed help with things.

If you are schooling your kids and taking care of a family member, you can do this! Every year is different for us because of the age of each kids. When there is work the kids can do on their own, I will save that work for when we go to my mom's house. Or, if there is a video for them to watch, I will put it on while I get things done.

I am learning to just stick with what they need to learn and things they are interested in. If I try to do too much in one year, we will all get overwhelmed and not enjoy school as much as we could.

Gentleness Class

Every once and a while my kids would do something that would hurt my mother. They were not trying to, she just gets hurt easily and they sometimes forget to be gentle. There have been times they hurt me too. One of my kids may have broken my nose when jerking their head up suddenly during a bath.

One time my daughter, Lila thought it would be funny to scare her Meemaw. So when my mom came out of her restroom, Lila said "Boo!" It caused my mom to collapse. Thankfully, she was right next to her bed and fell partly on the bed. Lila thought Meemaw was just playing and came to tell me how good she is at scaring people. When I went into the room, Meemaw was not responding. After a while, Lila realized Meemaw was not joking around. She sobered very quickly and went to the other room, sat on the couch, and put her head on her knees. After I took care of Meemaw, I made sure my daughter knew the importance of not startling older people. I also did my best to assure her that she wasn't a naughty girl, she just needed to be careful with others.

Take Away

Being a parent can be hard. Seeing your parents grow old is not easy. It can be tricky raising kids while helping your parents (or siblings, etc). It can feel like a tightrope or tug-of-war. Every family is different, so you will need to look at the different needs of the people you are caring for and come up with a plan that fits. It will not all be easy, but you got this! Have a plan and keep to it. Do not give up. There is a song that I love so much, sung by Mary Mary, called Can't Give Up Now. It is totally worth listening to. God used this song and the ladies who sang it to really help me in some struggles I've had. Now, how can God use you to enrich others?

Some situations call for outside help. If that is you, there is no shame in receiving or needing help. Sometimes God uses our weaknesses to help strengthen our faith and character. I will be talking about needing physical help in this next chapter.

6

Caring While Needing Care

Wake Up Call

After I had my third daughter Lila, I started having severe health problems. I was unable to sing to my new baby or specials at church, because of my throat. I would lose my voice and get a lot of tonsil stones. I would randomly get lightheaded and have chest pains. Let's just say, I had a lot of different symptoms and no answers about the cause.

One day, right outside Mikayla's room, I started having chest pain and couldn't say anything that made sense. My legs started giving out. Next thing I knew, I was on the floor and could hear my dad talking. I honestly thought I was going to see my Maker that day. After a while, not sure how long, I was finally able to talk. I have seizures when I am around acetone fumes. This experience was a little like a seizure. The only difference was I could hear the people around me. I just wasn't able to move.

That was my wakeup call! I had to do something drastically different if I was going to be around long enough to see my kids graduate. My mom had given me a book called Living on Live Food. It said that when we cook food, the heat kills some of the nutrients. So, I went on a

40-day raw, vegan diet. The first few days were horrible, but a few days later I started feeling better. About a month into it I felt like a super star! When the 40 days were over I started eating some cooked food in the afternoons. I ate healthy things that would help me be the best mom and daughter I could be.

Just like my mother's health affected me, my health affects my kids. When I am not feeling good I cannot do as much with them. When I don't feel well, I am not as pleasant to be around. In order for me to take good care of others, I have to also take good care of myself. I have a better chance of giving great care when I feel my best. Eating right and getting enough rest is important for thinking clearly and displaying grace and kindness.

Thanksgiving Surprise

I was back to mowing the lawn, running around with my kids, help-ing my mom, and it felt wonderful! That Thanksgiving I had so much to be thankful for. In our house, we usually host my parents, aunts, brothers and their kids for a lunch or dinner get-together. Everyone usually comes to my house, because we have the most space.

We started taking turns saying what we were thankful for. I said something about my good health and that I was thankful for not being pregnant or nursing... Little did I know I had a very small bundle waiting to be discovered!

The next month, on December 23rd I told my husband we were going to have another baby. That was a roller coaster of emotions for me. It had been four years exactly since I had lost my heaven baby. That was the same day I was planning on telling him about baby number two. All day long I relived that day four years before and prayed this Christmas would be different. All day I went back and forth between trusting in God and having unexpected fear and sadness. Thankfully, the day came and went without any blood or cramping!

Stocking Decor

We also host people at my house on Christmas, so I thought it would be a good time to do a fun baby announcement. Before all the family members started coming in, I hung up a baby-size stocking next to the rest of ours and so no one could miss it, I placed a pacifier on the outside of it. Well, guess what? They missed it! Quietly I waited for someone to say something. About an hour later, I asked if anyone noticed anything special! It took a while before someone asked if I was having another little elf. If you have a family who is unobservant, hopefully this helps you feel better!

Contraction!

I was still feeling pretty good physically for a few weeks into my pregnancy, but then my stomach started doing its thing! I wound up in the ER to get rehydrated. I eventually started to eat things I hadn't in over a year, because I couldn't keep healthier foods down. That felt like such a long pregnancy! I was sick until about half way through. Then, the entire last month I was in labor. No joke, about four weeks of contractions every five minutes that would last a minute and a half. Day and night!

It was not always pleasant having contractions while reading or cooking for my kids. Sometimes my mom would let my children nap at her house. My aunts would watch them sometimes when I would go to the doctor or hospital. It was nice having family close by to help here and there, but I still had a responsibility to my kids. I needed to show them love even when I am in pain. That can be tricky sometimes. When I'm hurting, I don't feel like being social! When you have small kids, you have to put their needs ahead of your wants.

A month of contractions can be testing, to say the least! I found Phil Roberson and his sons' voices soothing. I would just zone out with their podcast, Unashamed while playing Dr Mario! Long story short, I finally had another healthy baby. It was another beautiful girl we named Audrey Grace.

Life can be what you make it. I can dwell on the hardships of life. There are enough of those to go around. Or, I could remember the overwhelming grace of Christ. Yes, I had a rough pregnancy, but God lovingly helped me through it. His grace outweighs any possible situation I go through, even the situations in these next chapters.

Are You Ready to Die?

A couple years after Audrey was born, I started having severe health problems again. This time, it was time to visit a gastroenterologist, need I said more?! In the span of one year, I had to go to the ER four times, a couple different types of doctors, and an urgent care center twice. Again, I wasn't getting any answers, which was very frustrating.

Once again, I thought it was the end of my earthly life. I wound up bringing Mikayla close to me one day and told her how much I love her and advised her to live for Jesus. This was a rough situation. I hated not being able to do the things I should do with my children. It felt like déjà vu, but this time I was the mom.

I truly believe this part of my life was what I needed for my relationship with God to grow strong again. I needed to look at the legacy I was leaving to my kids. I needed to understand where my focus was at the time and where it should have been. The good thing about coming to the point of death or caring for someone who is to that point, is you start to ask important questions.

These are some of the questions I would like for you to ask yourself:

- What will happen to my soul if I die right now? Am I truly right with Jesus?
- What will happen to my family when I die? What can I do to help them succeed when that happens?
- What will people remember most about me? Will they use words like kind, forgiving, and generous or words like self-centered and cranky?

Is my focus on things that are praise worthy and long lasting? Or am I focused on things that are a waste of time and don't have any true value?

Bowels, Don't Fail Me Now!

My intestines and I have never been very good friends! On my last trip to the ER the doctor suggested I have my gastroenterologist check to see if I had a certain autoimmune disorder. She told me I was my own best advocate and that I should keep taking notes and doing research. When I did the one-week post-hospital follow up with my Gastroenterologist, he would not test me for that particular disorder, because it was so rare, and they just needed to find the right medication combo that would work for me. Needless to say, I have not returned to that doctor!

Don't get me wrong, I'm not against all doctors. There are a lot of doctors and nurses who truly care and are very helpful. But this particular doctor was determined to keep me on high dosages of medication the rest of my life. They wanted to treat the symptoms without knowing the cause. No, thank you!

I started doing my own research on the disorder and found out I had every symptom listed. It was like I was reading my exact situation and things were making a lot more sense. After making a few adjustments to my diet, sleeping routine and supplements, I am starting to improve. Thank you, Lord!

At first, I thought the doctor was an idiot for handling my case the way he did. Okay, I might still think that! But I now see, I do the same thing sometimes with other issues. When I am faced with things that are emotionally tough to deal with, it is so easy to ignore it and hope the problem fixes itself. I can just play Dr. Mario while listening to a podcast to help me ignore the problem. If you do that long enough with the wrong medication you will die. You have to find what the real issue is and use the right treatment if you are wanting to be healed completely.

So often our real issue is us, but who wants to admit that? Usually, I don't like the problem being me, because I hate the taste of humble pie! It takes a lot of courage to be humble. When I admit to God and to myself that I need help, it can be very humbling. I like doing things on my own.

When I worked with Teen Missions the guys who worked on land crew would say I have the strength of ten men. I earned that reputation by working hard. It was something I took a lot of pride in. That was the problem. God doesn't want to knock me down a few pegs because He has something against strong women. He allows me to go through periods of weakness so He can show me the courage of humility.

It was only when I was humble with the Lord that He was able to show me what true strength looks like. When we go to Him during our difficulties and are willing to be His students, He is able to renew us and give us a better life (Matthew 11:28-30).

The Ultimate Caregiver

One day a few months ago, I was really struggling with if I was ever going to be completely healed and if God was ever going to change my mom's situation. In the midst of my struggle, I heard a song that I later learned was sung by Natalie Grant called More Than Anything. The part that spoke to me was her asking God to help her want the Healer more than the healing. Then she asks for Jesus to help her want Him more than anything.

The reason God wants us to submit to Him, is because that is the only way we can have complete healing. He is the only treatment for so many of the things we try to ignore. We do not have to be perfect when we know and are known by the perfect Savior. When we give God authority in our lives it takes the stress off of us. When we give Him our time and effort, He is able to complete us like no other "treatment" can. You do not have to manage everything alone; He loves you and He is the ultimate Care Giver.

Some days we may have to humble ourselves to other humans, like when we cannot stand up because of feet or intestinal pain. Take courage, my dear friend, it shows more strength than you think to be able to ask for help. And it shows wisdom when you stop ignoring issues to surrender and allow Jesus to heal you internally. You may not always receive your bodily healing that you wish for, but I pray you find completion that only He can give.

Side note, it is good to do your own research, because not all doctors care about you like they do their paycheck. They also cannot see and feel everything you are going through. It can help the person taking care of you when you take notes of what is going on. Get medical help when needed, but be sure to take notes and/or ask for a summary of diagnosis and treatment given. If you are the one helping someone else, take notes for them on what is going on and all medicine taken.

Love in Action

I cannot save my mom from every pain she faces, but I can show her the love of Christ. Actions say more than your mouth ever will. As we invite Jesus to work with us (and on us) the more we will be like Him.

The Bible says that God is love. It also goes into detail of what love is. (1 Corinthians 13:4-7)

Love IS:
Patient
Kind
Considerate
Truthful
Hopeful
Durable

Love is NOT:
Envious
Boastful
Arrogant
Rude
Selfish
Irritable
Resentful

The more we are like Christ the better care we can give.

Need Vs Deserve

We all have things we need healing from. Most of the time healing has a treatment plan that isn't always pleasant. I will talk about some of that in chapter 7. God knows what we need and has done the heavy lifting for us to get it. He died a very painful death in order to save us from an eternity without Him. He went through horrible, undeserved treatment to heal our undeserving souls. He received the pain we deserved so we can receive His grace and mercy. We may not always feel like it, but He is always looking out for us and wants what is best for us, even if it means going through a painful recovery.

7

Triple Bypass

Discouraged

At this point in life, I had four daughters, and I would go to my mom's house to help her when she needed me and when Adam could help me with the kids. My mother's neuropathy was so painful she could barely lift a spoon to her mouth or get dressed. Every time I would go to her house, I would make sure she had some ice water and check if she would like for me to cook her anything.

By this point, food was an afterthought, and she was getting very discouraged by the 24/7 pain with little to no relief. I was getting discouraged for her. I wanted to hold on to hope, but I was only watching her get worse and was able to do less and less to help her.

If you are at the point of despair and you can't see things getting any worse, hold on! Don't give up. Cry out to Jesus. He never sleeps, He is always watching over us and listening to our pleas. Even when we do not feel or see His plan, He never stops working things together for good for the people who love Him (Romans 8:28). It doesn't say all things feel good. He says He will work them towards our good. Sometimes the work is hard and painful. Sometimes we have to wait for the good, but hold on. God is good no matter how bad the situation you find yourself in.

How To Clean Two Houses

Caregiving can be stressful at times. One thing I have done to help keep track of things is when I would clean my toilets, that would be the day I would clean my parents' toilets. The day I would dust and vacuum their house is the day I would dust and vacuum my house. This didn't always happen, but it helped me keep track of things better.

Some days I would do something at my house and would go to do it at their house, but she would be sleeping, and I didn't want to wake her. Some days I would do something at her house and run out of energy by the time I had gotten the girls to bed and would save it for another day. The trick is not to make excuses for laziness but give yourself grace when you have a lot going on.

You should not lay around all day because you don't want to do anything helpful. You also don't need to go without rest because your schedule is too full for sleeping. Get realistic with your time. Sleeping is more important than videogames. Your loved ones are more important than a movie. And your rest is more important than your kid having a different menu than everyone else.

We need unwind time here and there. Just make sure you have a healthy amount of it. Needs should come before preferences and entertainment. There is no shame in asking for help while you are helping others. Encouraging others to reach out and be a blessing is a great thing to do for a friend. Doing for others is one of the best remedies for depression. Sometimes depression needs medicine, but a majority of the time it needs a healthy diet and thinking outside of ourselves.

Food was made for our bodies, not our bodies for food. You should eat when your body needs food. And eat the foods that will make you feel good afterwards. I love ice cream with chocolate and peanut butter (and almost anything else with peanut butter!), but I know if I eat it at certain parts of the day or too much, I will not feel so great and have a long recovery period. I have to get real with myself and the foods I eat. I know I can't handle much sugar. Ice cream tastes so good while I am eating it, but afterwards I am in pain and not so useful to anyone. Some things are great in the moment, but is it worth the aftermath? That goes for more than just food. Some things seem like fun but have too high a price.

Brother Neighbor

About a year ago my brother, Blake moved onto the other side of my parents' house. It was nice being able to see him a little more often and have someone else be close by for my mom. Before this, I felt like my dad and I were the only ones able and willing to help my mother. Blake had been a help with buying some of her medications, but now he was around if she needed him to lift something heavy or give her a ride somewhere. This was perfect timing for what would happen a few months later.

March 2023
Hot Dog!

Because my mom couldn't really go anywhere and people didn't visit her, Blake thought a dog would be a good companion. He, my mom, and my daughter, Haley went dog searching. They found the sweetest dog and named her Clementine. The dog was already potty trained and was usually very calm. For a while I think Clementine gave my mom some distraction from the pain she was in. It helped give her something else to think about.

My girls loved going over and petting the dog and giving her chew toys. Eventually they got a good lesson on the importance of not leaving their own toys around where the dog could chew on them. Audrey was not happy when she found a couple of her dolls' limbs missing!

Having a dog also helped my kids have more to be responsible for. They would help walk and feed the dog in between school subjects. On days my mom's pain was too intense to be in the living room, we would bring our schoolwork to her house and dog-watch while we did schoolwork.

It gave us a change of scenery and the dog was a great reward. When someone would finish a subject, they could pet, feed or walk the dog. That was enough of a reward for them to be very motivated. I don't think that would work for every kid, but I am glad it worked for us!

April 2023

As we got close to the end of the school year, my kids would take longer and longer to finish their tasks. One day they surprised me by finishing earlier than ever, so I let Mikayla go walk Clementine. She came back a bit early and said something about Meemaw needing me outside. When I followed Mikayla to where my mom was, I found her leaning on a pole very pale and clammy with the dog leash around her wrist. Thankfully, Blake was home from work that day. I handed the dog leash to Lila, supported my mother's weight and sent Mikayla to get Uncle Blake. He helped me get her in a chair and eventually into his car. He gave her a ride to the hospital while my girls and I took care of Clementine and the outside cats.

Coincidence?

I am so thankful it was on a day my brother was off and available. If my mother would not have had the dog, she would have been inside and my daughter would not have had a reason to go over to her house at that time. That day was the only day in four months that my kids finished school early. I'm talking over two hours early that day! I'm telling you; God worked a lot together for us to find my mom in the time we did and get her to the hospital.

Heart Surgery

After a while of waiting at my parents' house with the dog and children, we found out that my mom needed to have something called Triple Bypass Surgery. She had already had stints put in a year or two before this and was having issues with some of them. In this surgery they would take three blood vessels from her leg and put them in her heart to help blood flow to blocked arteries. Because this surgery would help with blood flow, it would supposedly help with her neuropathy. Now that she was at the hospital, all we could do was wait.

Dog-Sit

She was at the hospital for about two weeks. While she was there my children and I dog-sat while home schooling at my parents' house. My husband and I are both allergic to dogs and cats so we couldn't bring her to our house. And because she liked to chew on random things we couldn't leave her there unsupervised.

My dad would come home for the night, so we would go to our house when he got home. When he would leave for the hospital we would go back to their house. Before we would go over in the mornings, I would bring the food we would need for lunch and dinner, and the papers and books we would need for school. While we were there, I would let each kid play with the dog when they would finish a subject. After Adam would get home the kids would go to our house with him, and I would clean and spend time with the dog until my dad would get home. Some nights Blake or his girlfriend would spend the night at my parents' house and watch the dog so my dad could stay at the hospital with my mom.

Sometimes care giving is taking care of pets or plants so others can care for a person. Sometimes, it's just doing things to take part of the load off of someone else.

When it comes to homeschooling while caring for others or moving around, it takes a little more thinking ahead. Just think of the things each person will work on, bundling the kids in subjects like science and history so there are less classes to prep for really helps me.

Prep Work

Before my mom was able to come home, the house had to be clean, the restroom and her bed had to be sanitized, and the dog had to find a temporary home so she wouldn't jump on my mom. I made sure the house was clean and there were no tripping hazards, but I could not bring the dog in my house because of our allergies.

My Aunt Cindy let the dog stay with her for a few weeks. My kids would walk the dog for her while she was working. This worked for a little while, but eventually we had to get rid of the dog. This was very hard on my mom, because she felt like it was all her fault.

Home From Hospital

When my mom first got home, she was very sore. She was not supposed to reach up for anything or bend down. She wasn't able to stand for very long, but needed to walk for a little bit a couple times each day. The first week or two, she needed help taking showers and getting dressed. There were times my mom would feel bad about taking me from my kids and husband, but I saw it as a way of honoring my mother. I never wanted her to feel bad about me helping her. It wasn't just me blessing her, it was me giving back and serving Jesus.

I Can't Hear You

The surgery wound up helping with the pain in her feet and the pain medication helped with the pain in her hands for a while. That part of surgery went well. Unfortunately, when the doctor pulled the cord out of her throat, he cut part of her esophagus and made it to where she could not talk loud enough to be heard clearly.

It has been six months since her surgery, and she still has to yell in order for people to hear what she is saying. So the good news: she has blood flowing nicely and her feet do not hurt as much. The bad news: she has lost the ability to sing and talk well. Remember, singing is how she first got my dad's attention, and was another part of her that she had to lose.

I do not know why God allowed each of these things to happen, but I know He is working all things together for our good. She might need time to listen, and so her voice is temporarily out of service. I'm not sure if this is going to be temporary or permanent. I wish I had the answers for her and the answers for me. I do not know everything, but I do know that God loves my mother even more than I do and He is going to do something great with this situation.

Tricky Questions

Being a parent can be the biggest blessing you can have. It can also be the most challenging thing you can ever do. Sometimes my kids ask the hardest questions! This time it was Haley. One night when I went into her room to kiss her good night, I asked her if she wanted to pray or wanted me to. Instead of answering, she asked me some tricky questions.

Through tears, she said something like, "Why isn't God answering my prayers? I pray for Meemaw everyday and she still isn't better. Doesn't God care about Meemaw?" I did my best to answer, but these were tough questions. I said something like, "I know God is listening to you when you talk to Him, Honey. He loves you and loves Meemaw too. I'm not sure why He is allowing her to go through this, but I know He has a good reason. Maybe to teach her something. She might need this struggle to become more beautiful. Like a caterpillar needs to struggle to get out of it's pupa to become a butterfly. Whatever the reason, God is trustworthy every time." I continued the conversation by letting her know I was proud of her for caring so deeply for others.

(We had just gone over the life cycle of butterflies the week before having this conversation, so it is what inspired some of my response.)

No matter what my answer, the struggle is real, and it is not going away overnight. When you care about someone, and they are going through a hard time, it is painful to watch them struggle. It is painful to see my mom in pain and a struggle watching my daughters hurt for her.

Some days you may be like me and want the ability to do awesome things like touch the sick and make them better. No matter what we struggle with, God is faithful and is working things together for our good. Sometimes the only thing we can do is show His love to them and pray they see Christ when they look at us.

8

Saying Good-Bye... Again

Hard Question #2

As I was putting my six-year-old to bed one night, I was faced with another of the toughest questions I have ever been asked. "Is Meemaw going to die?" It took me by surprise, so it took a minute to answer.

I knew I had to be honest and tell her, "I don't know." That isn't always the easier thing to admit to my kids. (It's kind of like telling my husband he's right and I'm wrong!) Nonetheless, it was a conversation I had to face. I didn't want Lila to be sad, but I wanted her to be prepared.

I have always tried ending conversations with my loved ones with loving words, because we are not promised tomorrow. That is something I hope to instill in my girls. Treat others with loving care because if you don't, not only could you live with the regret later, but you rob them of feeling valuable. When you treat people this way, it will make you a better person and make them better as well.

Cut Open

As my mom recovered from her surgery, she needed extra help. Like I said, it takes a lot of humility to ask for help and it takes courage to be humble. Depending on others for mostly everything is a very vulnerable place to be.

When I was healing from my c-section it was very painful. It was rough, even when things were going well. So, when pain killers would wear off and I was in a non-air-conditioned room with people who didn't seem to care that I was just cut open, I got a bit irritable and had a hard time keeping my emotions in check.

That is something I had to remember when my mom came home from her triple bypass. She had been cut open in her chest and leg and had her throat messed with. She needed someone to take good care of her and be mindful of her needs. She needed someone to know what her limitations were and see that she stuck to them while being gentle and showing her respect.

Someone needed to be with her all the time at first in case she needed anything. My dad and I would take turns staying with her while the other went to church or took care of business. My dad would help with most meals, I would help her shower and do laundry, and we both would help change bedding every three days. As time went by, she was able to do more and more by herself and instead of someone being with her all day I would just go over when she would text me.

Do What's Needed
Having someone around all the time can sometimes be annoying. Think of what you would want if you were that person. Having someone ask every 10 minutes what you need is just about as annoying as the beeping noise the hospital beds make!

Having to remind someone that the sheets need changed every time can make someone feel unloved, especially if it's a woman you are caring for. Don't wait to be asked every time before doing things you know need done. Having to ask for a meal every time, and the sheets every three days, and the laundry every day would make anyone more vulnerable. They are already vulnerable enough without having to ask for the obvious every time.

I wrote things on my weekly planner so it would help me remember to help her every other day with a shower and every three days to change sheets. My dad was able to take off for a while and was able to be there for her, but didn't always think like a caregiver. This is something Adam and my dad have in common. Some people are natural caregivers while others don't always know what to do when taking care of someone.

If you are not a natural caregiver, there is no need to feel shame. Here are some things that might help:

When the doctor gives a list, write it down or ask for it on paper. Then follow the instructions. For example; when my mother had her heart surgery the doctor told me the house needed to be clean, the restroom needed to be sterile, and there needed to be no tripping hazards. I made sure I cleaned the restroom very well, I cleaned the house of any possible things she could trip on and made sure everything was wiped clean with no dirty laundry or dishes anywhere.

The doctor told me my mom would need to shower every other day and have the sheets cleaned every three days. I am a paper kinda girl so I wrote on my calendar every thing for every day so I would be less likely to forget. If you are a phone type of person, I would set alarms for the things that need to be done. When a person is recovering, they might not think of those things and they shouldn't have to, because they have you.

Unless the doctor says otherwise, everyone needs to eat. Most people eat three times a day and need plenty of liquids. You can set an alarm or just fix food for the person when you fix food for yourself. After every meal clean the messes that were made. It can be very discouraging to have to clean up a mountain of dishes when getting over a surgery or illness.

When you see their cup is running low, fill it (unless the doctor has limited their fluid intake).

Make sure to check on them from time to time, do not wait for them to yell for you. And when you do something for them, do not rush. This is a ministry opportunity, a way to be a blessing and show someone love. I have had nurses look like they are running a marathon and it made me not want to ask them for anything, even when I needed something. I have also had nurses that make me feel like I was their most important patient and it made me feel special. That is the type of service I challenge you to give.

If you are not sure what you can do to help, don't silently wonder. Ask.

Voice Or Feet?

My mom was starting to improve and was looking great. She had been dropping excess weight and the incisions were healing nicely. Her feet were not as painful so she was able to wear shoes again, praise the Lord! The one thing that she could not do now was talk (and maybe join a wrestling team!). That was tough. It was like she had traded in her voice for her feet. Singing is what had first gotten my father's attention and now she could barely talk to him. This has been a difficult thing for her to experience.

It took a while for my children to understand that Meemaw wasn't yelling at them to be mean, she was just trying to make her voice loud enough for them to hear her. Most people cannot hear her over the phone, so it makes it very difficult to get business done.

One lesson with this is, just because a person looks good and seems to have everything going for them, doesn't mean they feel good and don't have problems. Another lesson to this is sometimes God needs us to be quiet while He works on healing our hearts. Did that sound too cheesy? Regardless, sometimes we just need to give up talking for a while in order to learn and grow. We do not always have to give our opinion, but we should always show love.

Real Christ Follower

I have one thing I would like to say to church goers before I move on. I missed a fare amount of church during this process. Sometimes it would be because I was watching a dog. Other times, I was staying with my mom so she wouldn't be alone. I gave up "synagogue time" so I could be obedient to God.

The Bible never says, "Thou must go to church every week." or "You have to fellowship with other believers in a designated building in the denomination you chose." But, the Bible does say that if you know to do good and do not do it, that is considered sin (James 4:7). It says to love one another (1 John 4:7). It says to give generously (1 John 3:16-18). When someone asks you to go one mile, go two (Matthew 5:41). Another way to say this is, if my mom asked me to wash a load of laundry, I could fold it as well. The whole point of this is to do more than asked or what is expected of us. When you do this, it will make you the best employee. It will make the people around you feel special. It will make the world a better place.

Church is a great place to learn about God and spend time with some wonderful people. I know some of you have had great experiences going to church. For those of you who haven't, I'm so sorry. I do encourage you to find a good, Christ centered church, but make sure you are placing church in the spot it should be. God did not intent on church being a popularity club. He does not want it to take His place. He should be Lord (aka Authority) and the church should be a group of people helping encourage and bring people closer to the Lord.

We should never feel bad about missing a sermon on the weekend when we are showing the love of Christ to someone. We should not let church be our connection to God. That is why Christ died, so we could have a direct line to Him.

Head Butt

Sometimes when someone is healing it is easy to forget to be gentle. Lila forgot to be gentle one day when giving her Meemaw a hug. She went in a bit too swiftly and wound up hitting my mother's chest with her head. It took my mother a while to catch her breath. She ended up hurting for days. It wasn't intentional or the hardest collision, but open-heart surgery takes a long time to heal from.

Gentleness is not something that comes naturally to most. It is something that must be learned. If you are taking care of someone, gentleness and patience are two things you will need to put into practice. And something you must teach any child that is with you.

Complete healing only can happen if you give the amount of rest required. I learned this the hard way when I had first joined staff at Teen Missions. I had sprained both my wrists (and broke one of them) when I was doing a trick while roller skating. A little over a month later I was running the obstacle course at boot camp with my team. My wrists were feeling just fine and I had just stopped wearing the wrist braces, so

I totally forgot not to put too much pressure on my wrists. I jumped for the rope at the slew and immediately got an overwhelming pain down my left arm. To this day (over twelve years later) I have issues with my wrists, because I did not wait for them to completely heal.

One lesson here is, just because there is no brace or outward scar doesn't mean there isn't pain and internal healing happening. On a very practical note, if a doctor advises you to not lift things for 6 weeks, you wait at least six weeks. Then slowly get back into a healthy routine. Our bodies are made to do some amazing things, but we do still have limitations. Be wise with what you have been given and have patience while healing.

Good Night, and Good Bye

We thought my mom was out of the woods... Until I got a phone call from my cousin, David one night that an ambulance was on its way to my mom's house. Her blood pressure was acting up and we all knew this was the last night we'd have with my mom.

We said how much we loved her. She told me she was proud of me. We made her as comfortable as we could. We all gave our hugs and kisses before saying our last "good night."

Part of me was so relieved for her, she had been going through so much for so long. She would finally not be in any pain and stop having to go to hospitals. She wouldn't have to think of finances anymore.

The next day, I prepared what I would say to my kids. I waited for the call from my dad, and instead got a text from my mom. I had a mix of emotions. At this point, I mostly had just been looking at what needed to be done. I wasn't thinking of how things made me feel.

I had to go from helping my mom get better, to planning how to help my dad with things when she was gone, to helping my mom get better again. Most of the time I managed to stuff feelings and "get 'er done." Every once and a while overwhelming feelings would burst forth and I would need to physically stay active in order to handle them.

It is hard watching the people we love hurt and go through pain. Sometimes we need to bottle emotions temporarily to get things done, but eventually we need to work through our grief in an appropriate, healthy way. There is no shame in getting help from a psychiatrist or a trusted wise person you know.

God made more than one person so we could talk to each other, pray for one another, and help each other out (James 5:16, 1 Thessalonians 5:16, Luke 22:31-32). We should put God first (Proverbs 3:6), but there are times we need others to hug and talk to. Sometimes we need people to mourn with us or laugh with us. Romans 12:15 advices to mourn with those who mourn and rejoice with those who rejoice. This doesn't mean ignore your emotions. Some days we need to help others deal with their issues first, but mourning with someone is listening to them, waiting with them and supporting them while they grieve.

9

This is the Song that Doesn't End...

Pain on Hold

Even though she could not talk and her chest was hurting from surgery, it was so good seeing my mom's feet and hands back to normal for a little while. After a short time, my mom's hands started flaring up again, but she was still able to put shoes on and get out of the house.

She was able to go shopping and look around at the thrift store with me. That was so refreshing. I felt so much relief for her. One day my mom and I just sat outside watching the kittens play. She was still recovering from surgery, but her shoes were not the torture devises they had been before the surgery. That was such a relaxing day and a wonderful memory. I was really looking forward to my mom being able to live that better life that I had been praying and waiting for.

The pain in her feet stayed away for a few months, but then started its comeback. Gradually, it started getting severe again. This was so disheartening. It was nice for her to have a reprieve of some kind, but I was not throwing a welcome party for this neuropathy pain.

Never Ends

My kids like driving people crazy with the song from Lamb Chops that keeps repeating itself! That can get pretty irritating. Especially those moments they decide to sing it when I am already in an emotionally weak point.

Sometimes hardships hit us when we need them the least. Sometimes it feels like this chapter of our life will never end (or keep repeating itself). It feels like my mom will never be healed or be called to the next life. Oh, will this ever end?!

My heart breaks daily for her. I can't take her pain away. I can't ease her burden. But I do know the One who has said in Matthew 11: 28-30 that we can give our burdens to God and He will walk with us and help us with our heavy load. He is not a thief though, we must give Him those burdens. He won't always remove the burdens, but He can lighten the load and strengthen us along the way.

There are days I do not know how to console my mother. I feel helpless and sometimes useless. At times, I have found myself withdrawing in order just to emotionally survive. It is okay to seclude yourself every once and a while to pray and regroup. Jesus did it Himself, but then He went right back into ministering to others. (Luke 5:16) There is a reason God made a day of rest for each week. We need to regularly be renewed, with our bodies and minds. Then, after we get the nourishment and rest our bodies need, we go back to helping others.

To be completely honest, this is the hardest chapter for me to put on paper, which means it will probably be the most helpful for some people reading. So here I go... there are times I just want it to end.

I love my mother more than I could express and hate seeing her hurt. I hate feeling powerless to truly help her. And there are days I get angry and hurt by the Lord because He could do something, but for some reason chooses not to. That sometimes makes me mad.

I do not know why God has not healed my mother. I do not know why He hasn't taken her off this earth. At times I feel like it would be the most merciful thing He could do. But I am making the choice to trust that He knows what He is doing (or not doing) and has my and my mother's best interest in mind. Though it may not be immediate, He has our eternal good in mind.

Fact Or Feeling

My daughter Haley does not do well with red or yellow food dye. It's like she has no control over herself when she consumes it. Therefore, I do my best to not give her any! My daughter, Audrey is highly allergic to peanut and sunflower seeds. If it gets on her skin she breaks out. so I do not let the other kids eat it while sitting next to her. It's because I love them that I withhold those things from them. God sometimes withholds things from us out of love.

There have been times my children see other kids having certain treats that they are not allowed to have and feel left out. They sometimes might think I am not a cool mom for withholding things from them. Sometimes they get mad at me.

Sometimes Audrey might think I like her sisters more for giving them peanut butter and her almond butter. You and I know why I withhold that type of nut butter she asks for, but she is still young and doesn't fully understand the consequences of me giving in to her request. When she was really little, she did not understand. Even now, she knows I'm just looking out for her, but she wants the yummy looking treat. Not long ago she asked me, "Mom, are you sure I'm allergic to peanut butter?" Even though peanut butter tastes better than almond butter (in my opinion), there are times my other daughters want the special stuff I give to Audrey.

I sometimes don't understand why God is not giving me what I am asking for. Sometimes it makes me mad. I do not understand now why my mom is going through this, but someday God will let me know. Neuropathy pain and peanut butter might be totally unrelated, but the parent's love is very much the same.

My children may not always feel like I love them or have their back. Sometimes, when I answer yes to one person's request and not theirs, they feel like I must love the other person more. But just because their feelings tell them something, doesn't mean it's true. The same goes for us. We might feel like our Heavenly Father doesn't care, but that doesn't mean it's true.

Switching Plates

It's easy to think our problems are worse than someone else's. We might want to switch some of the items on our "plate" with someone else. We may even think we are doing our best and it can't get any worse. I want to encourage you right now not to take feelings or thoughts as truth. Feelings come and go, but God is the only thing that will never change. Not because He's lame or not up to date, but because He is solid and reliable. He knows what each of His children need to grow and not get sick. Are we going to try to sneak the "butter" from someone else's plate or trust our heavenly Father?

I do not make my kids do school because I want to take away their play time. I do not have them answer challenging questions to watch them fail. I want them to learn and exercise their brains every week so they can become smart women who know how to figure things out and succeed in life. God does not want to watch my Mom fail or take away her joy. Some of the pain she is in is because of poor eating chooses from her past, and God knows why else.

I can still be frustrated for her and wish she could be pain free. When I get mad at the situation, I need to remember that God knows why (or why not). He sees the pain. He sees the situation. Whether He gives into my requests or not does not mean He loves me or my mom more or less. I cannot live off of feelings, they will not last. There is a hymn I love by Edward Mote that says,

"When darkness veils His lovely face I'll rest on His unchanging grace
In every high and stormy gale my anchor holds within the veil
On Christ the solid Rock I stand
All other ground is sinking sand."

Can't Out-Do

God is the ultimate Care Giver. We cannot care more, give more, love more, endure more. That doesn't mean we should sit around all depressed because we'll never be #1. Quite the contrary. We should let this motivate and inspire us.

Christ did not become a man to sacrifice Himself so we could be happy. He made that loving sacrifice so we could be complete and actually know God, obtain His love and have His Holy Spirit live in us. Now, that is amazing!

When you are at your point of not being able to do/handle more, give the rest over to God. Just because it might not look like He is working on the situation doesn't mean He isn't. Just like my wrist (that He was trying to heal before I messed it up), we don't always see the healing process.

We have our limits. We can do what's possible and let God do the impossible. When it looks like He is choosing to not do what you plan, know that His plan is far better. Even though He might not take the pain away, doesn't mean He doesn't care.

Verses

Here are some verses that have helped me through the "song" that feels like it will never end:

I can be content because He will never leave me or forsake me. (Hebrews 13:5)

God will never change. (His standards and love included) (Hebrews 13:8)

I can cast all my cares on Him, because He cares for me. (1 Peter 5:7)

Songs

Some songs are pretty annoying, but others can actually be very comforting and remind us of God's love and goodness. Here are a couple songs that have helped me in this chapter I have been facing:

How Deep the Father's Love for Us by Stuart Townend
(This one reminds me of how much Papa God loves my mom and will do what is best for her.)

Can't Give Up Now sung by Mary Mary
(This one says God has not brought us so far to leave in the mist of hardship. It says the Bible doesn't say there will never be struggles. So, when there are struggles, we need to ask God for strength.)

There are many more verses and songs that have encouraged and challenged me along my life's journey. It would take more than just one chapter to even mention them all, but I want to encourage you to use your God-given abilities to help others.

No matter how small it may seem to you, it could make the biggest difference in the life of the person you are doing it for. You could sing a song to some down cast soul. You could give a ride to someone who needs transportation. You could even make a glass of ice water to a woman with neuropathy.

10

Last and Least

Taking Smack

Usually you will hear "last, but not least," but this chapter is called Last AND Least. This world has been infiltrated with the thought that we have to look out for ourselves and don't take smack from anyone.

There is a time and place to not take smack and there is a time to simply be humble and let things go. For example, if one of my children were to be rude and demand something, I would not be doing them any favors by rewarding them for their rude behavior. In that situation, I should correct them and give them what they need. There's also the example of, if you are at work and a customer is having issues, you wouldn't tell them to suck it up and move on with their life. At least, I hope you wouldn't do that!

There is a time and place for things. We need to think of others, not just ourselves. In most cases, we should put others first. I want to be careful with saying this, because there are cases where you would need to speak up or step up. I once heard a family psychiatrist (Live On Purpose TV) say something that really helped my parenting. He advised to have just these three rules in your home:

1. Respect yourself and others
2. Respect property
3. Obey/Participate, unless it breaks rules 1&2

This really has helped me teach my kids that they need to show love and respect for others. If someone is doing something that is violating them or is messing up someone else's property they do not have to go along with it, because it breaks rules 1&2. If someone asks them for help and it's not putting them in danger, they should help the person and go the extra mile. If it puts them in a compromising situation, they should walk away (and in some cases seek help).

Last

Not only is this the last chapter, but it is the position we should put ourselves. The Bible says to not consider ourselves more highly than we should (Romans 12:3), and it says in Philippians 2 that we are to be like Jesus, who humbled Himself to the point of death on a cross. We are to put others' needs as more important than our wants and look out for those around us.

Not their wants, their needs. Some parents and spouses have a hard time with this. We need to look at what is going to be best for the other person now and in the future, not just what they, or we, want in the moment. Christ died to save us from death and the power of death, not to make things comfortable and easy for us. He wants us to live a full life and that should be our desire for ourselves and for those around us. A full life can only happen with Jesus. (John 1:4-5, 1 John 1)

Giving my kids sugar every time they start whining might help them not annoy me as much at that moment, but in the long run it is going to give them a sugar addiction and make them think whining is the way to get what they want. That is not the message I want to send to my kids. That is a selfish move (and not a wise one in the long run), because it's only thinking of how it affects me at the moment. Instead, I should think of their future and only reward good behavior and correct them (in an appropriate way) when they do wrong.

Best is Not always Easy

Just now, while I was typing, I heard my four-year-old messing with my six-year-old while they were supposed to be taking a nap. The thing that would have been easiest for me would have been to just ignore them and keep typing. What do you think would be best for them?

I know they both need rest because the six-year-old is just getting over an ear infection and their bodies are still growing. I also know they probably wouldn't get that rest if they are in the same room. So, I took my four-year-old into my room, laid with her for a few minutes to settle her down and let her know I still care.

If I wouldn't have interfered, I could have gotten more done, but they wouldn't have gotten what they needed. Parents, let's think of what is best for our kids not just what they want or what is easiest.

Serving Ideas

For those of you who are not parents thinking this does not apply to you, please wait! It can apply to everything. If you are a husband and you are tired from a long day at work, you could go relax and watch football, or take a few minutes to make your wife feel special and let her know you love her and think she looks beautiful. (Hopefully that is true!)

If you have a disabled sibling and the only companion they have seen all day is their television, you could spend time talking with them and make them a healthy meal.

If you have a neighbor who is stuck on the couch because of surgery, you could make them a meal and basket of things to do on the couch.

A friend of mine is a full-time caregiver to her husband who has Alzheimer's. One thing that could really help her is someone every so often hanging out with him so she can have a couple hours to herself. Care giving can be so fulfilling, but when you are doing it all day and night without much relief it can be exhausting. Another thing that could help her is someone helping with things around her house that her husband would have normally helped with.

I know it is not always convenient to go out of our way, but it can be very satisfying and is how we can obey God while making the world a better place. We can encourage others and help make their burden feel less burdensome. (1 Thessalonians 5:11, Galatians 6:2) These are only a few ideas, but I hope you get some inspiration from them of what you could do for the people God places in your life.

Hydrate and Hygiene

Please do not misunderstand me, we still need to take good care of ourselves. We need to have good hygiene, eat right and have our daily reflection time with the Lord. We never should feel guilty about those things. When you are well hydrated and don't smell like a wet diaper, you can be more pleasant to be around and better able to do more for the people around you.

Least

The title of this chapter is Last and Least. I explained the Last and now I'll explain the Least. The Bible says, the first shall be last and the least will be great. (Matthew 19:30) This does not mean to be the last to volunteer and the person who does the least! It means, God blesses the humble. When we think of ourselves less and others more, it shows humility and maturity.

It is better to be humble and others praise you than you to "toot your own horn" and be called out on things you can't really do. Luke 14:7-11 is a parable about someone who is choosing where to sit at a wedding. If you choose a VIP spot, you could get asked to move to a less important place. In other words, being put in your place! It would be much better to take the less important place and someone ask you to move to a better spot.

You're Somebody!

I don't want any of you to think that you are worthless, because you were made in the image of God! He values you enough to have made you and die for you. He is perfect and He would not have done that for a piece of junk. You are precious to Him and He cares greatly for you. He doesn't want us to be depressed about our looks, our smarts, or past. He made you the way He made you and He doesn't make mistakes. You are no more or less important than anyone else. We are to be humble, but please know that you are valuable to God. That means you are valuable!

He knew you would not be perfect, yet died for you anyway. That tells me that we don't have to worry about our background, our looks, or our intelligence. He can use anyone. He can and will give us the abilities we need to do what He asks us to do. He will never ask us to do anything that is not for our good and the good of those around us. We might not understand how things could be good for us, but God knows how to use it for our eternal good.

No Comparison

I used to think I was fat. At that time, I wasn't. Looking back, I only thought that when I compared myself with the super skinny people I lived with. I thought I wasn't good at art, but that was when I compared myself to my very talented tattoo-artist brother. Just because I felt fat and untalented didn't make it true.

God gave my brother a different talent than He gave me. Neither of us is less valuable because of the type of art we are able to do. We are able to do different things because God wants us to do different things!

God made my body different than the people I lived with, and that is alright! He made us each unique for a reason. Some people might need to learn how to have more self control with food than others. Some might need to learn how to trust God even though they were not made to do as much as the people around them.

God made us all different, and that is a wonderful thing! We don't need to compare ourselves to other people, because God made them to do other things. He made us all to glorify Him and bless others. We can do that differently than the people He made different than us! Instead of crying about a disability, we could maybe use it as a way to inspire someone else. Instead of being mad that God put you in a certain situation/family, maybe ask yourself why He did that.

The grass might look greener in someone else's lawn, but they have their shortcomings and issues just like you and I do. The "treat" they got might look tastier than what is on your "plate," but the Father knows what you need and when you need it. Even though it may look like it at times, God doesn't play favorites. He loves us all and is willing to help us in the "lawn" we are in and give us the "butter" that's right for us.

There have been some rough things I have gone through and have seen. Instead of using those things as an excuse to hate people or wallow in self-pity, I can use it as a ministry tool and can better understand the people who have gone through similar experiences.

The things that I hated most about myself when I was younger are now the things my husband enjoys the most about me! As a parent, there are one or two things that might frustrate me about my kids. Those are probably the things God will use the most in their future. Take courage, you are not alone. We all have insecurities here and there. The thing that you are self-conscious about is probably something someone else would love to have. The thing that frustrates you most about yourself (or someone else) might be the thing God will use in the future to change lives.

Disappointed

When we wait to be handed everything, we will most likely be disappointed in life. But, when we strive to serve the people around us and make the lives of others better, we will find contentment and joy much easier. When our goal is outward focused, there isn't as much room for disappointment. You don't have to start with anything too huge, maybe just smiling at the person behind you in line at the grocery store as the cashier is ringing you up.

Quality Time

In addition to doing things for others, we need to remember to take time to have conversations with them. So simple, but in today's society we often forget about the people right in front of us.

I see a big difference when I take time to spend with others. It would be pretty lonely being home all day by myself. Sometimes when Adam gets off early, I go to my parents' house, do a little bit of whatever needs to be done, and spend a few minutes talking with my mom. It does us both good. I love that woman so much!

God did not put other people on the earth for us to ignore one another while looking at our cell phones. Phones can be good, but don't forget to spend quality time with the people right in front of you.

Prioritizing

While I'm on the subject of quality time, it is important to spend time with God. We can serve God by serving others. Just remember, you cannot have a relationship with someone you never talk or listen to. It is so easy to ask God for things and get mad when you don't get them. It is only when we spend time reading the Bible that we can get to know who God is and understand His love and justice. (If you have a hard time understanding it, ask a pastor or someone you trust who understands it. One thing that has really helped me understand the Bible more is reading it chronologically and listening to a podcast called Bible Recap with Tara-Leigh Cobble)

Right now, what has your heart? Matthew 6:21 says where your treasure is, there your heart will be. In other words, are you investing and valuing tangible stuff or people and eternity? We can still own material possessions, there's nothing wrong with wanting nice things. The question is, do I care more about my kids or the stuff around them? Do I care more about my husband or the car he drives? We need to take good care of what we've been blessed with and be thankful for what we have. Just make sure your love for others exceeds your love of things.

Every day we have hundreds of choices to make. From the food we eat to the goals we set. I cannot change the poor decisions I have made in the past. For a while I lived in regret of some of those decisions. But, everyday we are given is another chance for us to take the right path. I want to ask again, what do you want to be remembered for and what consequences are you willing to pay? This is something some don't want to think about because it requires change or guilt. Some people might get temporarily pumped and treat it like a New Year's resolution.

This book was not written to put anyone to shame or to gloat about my awesome care giving skills. I am not always caring in my heart. That is something God has been working on in me and continues to do as I make one choice at a time. We can't change our past, but we can work on our future by the decisions we make today.

What/who are you choosing to invest in? Who are you able to bless today? It can be as simple as giving someone a cup of water.

www.ingramcontent.com/pod-product-compliance
Lightning Source LLC
Chambersburg PA
CBHW070445130626
46553CB00006B/2289